Turn Away from Teasing

by Gill Hasson

illustrated by Sarah Jennings

It also shows you how to tell when you should stop teasing someone else!

It's not always fun to be teased. This book shows how you can deal with it.

What is teasing?

Teasing is making fun of someone. It could be making fun of the way someone looks, or the way someone says or does something. It could be making fun of the things someone likes or dislikes.

4

Turn Away from Teasing

by Gill Hasson

illustrated by Sarah Jennings

Franklin Watts
First published in Great Britain in 2020
by The Watts Publishing Group

All rights reserved.

Copyright in the text Gill Hasson 2020
Copyright in the illustrations Franklin Watts 2020

Series Editor: Jackie Hamley
Series Designer: Cathryn Gilbert

A CIP catalogue record for this book is
available from the British Library.

ISBN 978 1 4451 6611 7 (hbk)
ISBN 978 1 4451 6612 4 (pbk)

Printed in China

Franklin Watts
An imprint of
Hachette Children's Group
Part of The Watts Publishing Group
Carmelite House
50 Victoria Embankment
London EC4Y 0DZ

An Hachette UK Company
www.hachette.co.uk

www.franklinwatts.co.uk

FSC
www.fsc.org
MIX
Paper from
responsible sources
FSC® C104740

A person might not mean for their teasing to upset someone.
Perhaps they mean for it to be funny.
But teasing can become upsetting if it hurts someone's
feelings. And if someone asks for the teasing to stop,
but it doesn't, teasing can turn into bullying.

What it feels like to be teased

Being teased can leave you feeling embarrassed or ashamed. Your cheeks might burn and you might want to curl up into a ball. Or you may wish you could just sink into the ground.

When you're being teased, you might feel upset,
or even angry. Your head might fill up with angry thoughts
about things you want to say or do to get back
at the person teasing you.

Feeling bad and missing out

Being teased can also make you feel unsure about things, or bad about yourself. You might avoid doing some activities in case you do them differently from other people, or make a mistake, or get laughed at.

Ada doesn't like to read out loud in class. Other children tease her because she talks very quietly. Ada feels embarrassed and wants to hide.

Leon doesn't want to play in the park with his friends because he feels upset when they tease him about his trainers being old and cheap.

When you end up in trouble

Sometimes you might feel so cross and angry when someone teases you that you lose your temper with that person. This can end up with you getting into trouble.

Ben teases his sister Annie by copying everything she does, and he won't stop even after she's asked him. Annie gets cross. She shouts at Ben and chases after him.
Then Ben blames Annie for chasing him,
and she gets into trouble with Mum.

When you get left out

Teasing can be even more hurtful if other people join in with it. Sometimes people tease in this way by leaving someone out.

Harper always sits with Emily and Mia at lunchtime, but today they told her she can't sit with them. Emily said it was because they were sitting with Evan and Liam to talk about the drama club.

"How come you're too shy for the drama club?" Liam teased her. Harper felt really hurt.

Later on, Harper told Mia and Emily that she didn't like being teased for feeling shy, and that they made her feel really left out.

What can you do about being teased?

One way to deal with being teased is to make a joke of it. If someone teases you, you can laugh and say, "Very funny!".

You might not always feel that you can laugh it off, though. If you feel sad or angry about the teasing, that's not okay.

The good news is that if the teasing upsets you, you can do something about it. Sometimes, the person doing the teasing might not realise how much it bothers you.

So, be sure to tell the person that you do not like being teased, and that you want them to stop.

How to stick up for yourself

If you are feeling upset or angry because of being teased, remember that there is nothing wrong with YOU!

The person doing the teasing may see it as a game.
If you seem upset, they might keep playing it.
And if you get angry, you might get into trouble.
But if you don't react, the game is over.

One way to stop the game is to ignore the person teasing you. If this doesn't work, tell the person that you don't like the teasing and want it to stop. Try not to sound upset. Just speak in a strong voice, loud enough for others to hear. Then walk away and do something else.

The person might keep teasing and try harder to get a reaction. But the less you react, the sooner they're likely to give up.

Annie decided to ignore Ben when he copied her. He kept on doing it, so she told him firmly to stop it, loud enough for Mum to hear. Ben didn't want to get into trouble, so he stopped.

Practise speaking up

You could ask someone to help you think of things to say when you want to stick up for yourself. Then practise! You can practise with someone else, by looking in a mirror, or both. You can try saying things like:
"I don't like it when you say that or do that!",
"Stop it!", "That's mean!" or "That's unkind!".

The more you practise, the easier it will get to speak up calmly and strongly. Then you'll know just what to say and do when you need to stand up for yourself.

I'm a strong person! I'm a nice person!

When someone teases you a lot, it's easy to start feeling bad about yourself and who you are. You can also practise feeling good about yourself.

Tell yourself that you're a nice, strong person. Think about specific things you like about yourself. Maybe you're a great singer, or good at listening, or a fast runner.

If you start to have sad or bad thoughts, imagine those thoughts sliding straight off you. Then think good thoughts and let those thoughts fill your mind.

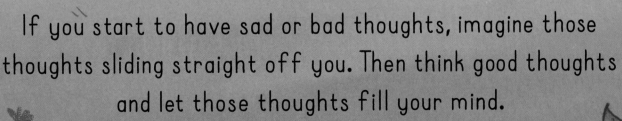

Talking about being teased

If the people teasing you will not stop, then it's time to talk about it with a grown-up you trust, like a teacher or someone in your family.

When you tell people that you're being teased, they might say things like "just play along" or "don't worry about it". They might tell you that if you do this, the teasing will simply stop.

Sometimes this does work. And if it does, that's great. But if the teasing continues, then getting advice like this is about as helpful as talking to a brick wall.

Getting help

If the person you talk to doesn't help you, talk to someone else—a grown-up you know and trust. This could be a parent, a grandparent, or an older sister or brother. Or it could be a teacher or a friend's parent. Make sure whoever you talk to knows how you feel about the teasing. Tell the person everything that is happening.

This sounds awful for you. Let's talk about what we could do about it.

...and I feel very upset and scared.

Perhaps you could ask your teacher to talk about teasing with the class: how it feels, and why it needs to stop when it becomes hurtful.

...and I don't like it.

We'll help you!

Your friends could help too. They can help you tell the people to stop teasing you.

If you don't feel you can talk to anyone you know, you can talk to someone on the phone. Look at page 30 to learn more about this.

Sticking up for others

What if you see someone else being teased or bullied? What can you do then?

When this happens, you might be afraid that, if you say something, you'll be picked on next. It's important to keep yourself safe, but if you see someone being teased unkindly or bullied, there are things you can do to help. Most people don't like it when someone is mean, and if you stand up for others, other people will probably be on your side.

You could try to stop it by saying something and getting your friends to speak up too. You could just say, "Don't be so mean!"
If the person does not stop acting mean, you or your friends could ask a teacher or an adult to help.

Two children at school were always teasing Kamil. They called him names and told him that he talked funny. Bella stood up for him. "It's mean to call Kamil names. Leave him alone!"

When the teasing didn't stop, Josh told the teacher and then asked Kamil to come and play with them instead.

If you tease others

Do you ever tease other children? Maybe you don't realise that you might be hurting their feelings.

One problem with teasing is that it's not always easy to know when to stop. But if you're teasing someone and they get upset or angry, you need to stop immediately and say you're sorry.

Try to imagine how you would feel if someone were doing this to you. You might think that you would just laugh about it, but not everyone can do that.

Look for other ways to have fun without embarrassing or upsetting someone else.

When teasing becomes bullying

Teasing can become bullying when it continues after the person being teased has asked for it to stop.

If you're teasing someone in a mean way, and you do not stop when they ask you to, then you are bullying them. If you encourage other people to tease someone, or if you don't let someone join in with you and your friends, this is bullying too.

Think about how you would feel if this was being done to you. If you believe you might be bullying someone, you may need help to understand why and to stop. Talk to a teacher or family member.

Turn away from teasing

If you're dealing with teasing, here's what you can do:

- Say you don't like it and tell the person teasing you to stop
- Refuse to react and ignore it
- Stand up for yourself if the teasing does not stop
- Practise what you will say so the words come easily to you
- Tell the person firmly, loud enough for others to hear, that you want the teasing to stop
- Stick up for others if you see them being teased. Other people will be on your side too.

If you're teasing someone and they get upset or angry, stop immediately and find other ways to have fun. Remember, teasing that upsets someone can become bullying.

If being teased is upsetting you, you don't have to deal with it on your own. Tell someone you trust what's happening to you. If you don't feel you can a talk to anyone you know for help, you can call ChildLine on 0800 1111, or go to www.childline.org.uk to sign up and send an email or post on the message boards. They will listen to you and give you some help and advice about what to do if you're being teased or bullied. You can also go to www.bullying.co.uk or phone them on 0808800 2222 or Kidscape: www.kidscape.org.uk for help and advice about what to do if you're being bullied.

Now you know what teasing feels like ...

... and what you can do to turn away from teasing!

Activities

These drawing and writing activities can help you to think more about how to manage teasing and bullying.

- Think of a time when someone has teased you. Draw a picture that shows what happened. At the bottom of the picture, write down how you felt about being teased. Which of these words would you use?
Cross, mad, annoyed, irritated, angry, bad, amused, wound up, sad, upset.

- Think of a time when you teased someone else. Draw a picture that shows what happened. At the bottom of the picture, write down how you think they felt about being teased. Which of these words do you think describes how they might have felt?
Cross, mad, annoyed, irritated, angry, bad, wound up, amused, sad, upset.

- Draw a picture of yourself. Draw a speech bubble coming from your head and write in it something you'd say to stand up for yourself if you were being teased or bullied.

- Make a list of all the things you like about yourself. Look in the mirror and tell yourself these things.

- If you were being bullied or you knew another child was being bullied, who could you talk to and ask for help? Draw a picture that shows you telling someone.

- Design an anti bullying poster. At the top of the poster you could write the words:
No bullying!

Then you could write these words and decorate the poster with drawings.
We will not bully others!
If we see bullying we will:
Speak up! Get help! Be a friend!

Notes for teachers, parents and carers

Most children will have experienced being teased by other children and adults. Often, when they're teased, children get embarrassed and upset or frustrated and angry. If your child is being teased, they need to know that it's okay to ask a grown-up for help. Talk with children about the idea that telling a grown-up about mean or upsetting teasing is not telling tales or tattling – it's not making a petty complaint or telling lies – it's telling you what's happening and asking for help to cope with it.

Children need effective techniques and strategies to help them take control. *Turn Away from Teasing* explains ways in which your child can do this. There's a number of strategies which you can help them with.
You can help them learn how to ignore and walk away from the teasing, and you can give them ideas for laughin it off. You can also help them to practise. The more practice you do at home in a non-threatening environment, the easier it will be for them to use the strategies in a more pressured situation.

What, though, if it's your child teasing others? You need to let your child know that it's not acceptable and that teasing can quickly turn into bullying. Talk with them about why they might be doing this – is there, for example, something that's frustrating them in their life and so they're taking it out on other children? Are they even being bullied themselves, by someone else?

If your child is being bullied or tells you that they know another child who is being bullied, it's imperative that they know they can come to you for help and support. Listen calmly and offer comfort and support. Children can hesitate to tell adults about bullying because they feel embarrassed or ashamed that it's happening, or worry tha their parents will be upset, angry, or reactive. Sometimes they're scared that if the child who's bullying finds out that they told, it will get worse. Others are worried that their parents won't believe them or do anything about it. Or they may worry that their parents will tell them to fight back when they're scared to. Praise your child for doir the right thing by talking to you.

Although your child can read this book by themselves it will be more helpful for both of you if you could read it together. Your child might want to read the book in one go. Others will find it easier to manage and understand if they just read a few pages at a time. Either way, there are lots of talking points. Ask your child questions such as Have you ever tried that? What do you think of that idea? How could that work for you?

Having read the book and helped your child identify some strategies that could work for them, you could come back to the book to remind yourselves of the ideas and suggestions for any future situations. If something didn't turn out so well, talk together about what they could have done differently. With patience, support and encouragement from you, your child can learn to cope with and better manage being teased. If, though, you're concerned that your child is being bullied, do talk to their school.

You can go to www.kidscape.org.uk. To phone their parent advice line call 020 7823 5430. You can also go to youngminds.org.uk or phone their parents' helpline free on 0808 802 5544. Or go to www.bullying.co.uk or phon their helpline on 0808800 2222. They have some useful articles too - simply put bullying into their search bar.